MW01291621

Zendesk Quickstart Guide

The Step-By Step Guide to Create ITIL Processes Quickly and Easily

By Crystal Taggart, MBA

About the Author

Crystal Taggart is a technologist and entrepreneur who has worked within both small startups and Fortune 500 companies. She's been working in technology as a developer and manager since 1997.

Her company, Atlas Innovations LLC based in Phoenix, AZ specializes in creating and implementing solutions that solve business problems.

Atlas Innovations recently launched their first product, TrainAsYouGo.com which is an online content management system that trains users as they navigate through the system.

Crystal has published multiple books including the Axure 7 RP Pro Quickstart Guide and The $6k Software Startup.

Copyright© 2014

Atlas Innovations LLC

Table of Contents

INTRODUCTION   4

CHOOSING THE EDITION   11

SETTING UP ZENDESK   13

GROUPS   13

SETTING UP SLAS   17

ADDING THE ON HOLD STATUS   18

MACROS   19

SETTING UP AUTOMATIONS   33

SETTING UP THE HELP CENTER   37

ADVANCED INTEGRATIONS   40

FAQS   45

CONCLUSION   47

Introduction

This book is short and sweet. It's about getting Zendesk implemented quickly and easily using ITIL best practices. Because Zendesk's training is pretty good, the goal was not to teach you how to use Zendesk. The goal was to write a book that would take the reader 1 hour what took me 3 days (and 17 years of experience!) to do. I knew the process I wanted to implement, but figuring out how to implement that process within Zendesk was a challenge.

It provides a little bit of a background on ITIL, a little bit of process information, and a lot of configuration information. It doesn't walk through administration settings that are unrelated to setting up an ITIL-based process (such as how to configure your own email address.)
This book is focused as a step-by-step guide on the best way to configure Zendesk to support four major ITIL (Information Technology Infrastructure Library) processes:

Incident Management

Release Management

Problem Management

Change Management

When configuring Zendesk to support these processes., it's important to keep in mind the holistic process for all the service processes and how those processes interact together. This book is a guidebook to set up the process, but will vary based on the organizational structure and needs of your own environment.

ITIL was created by the UK government as a means to govern their internal IT processes and procedures. This book is based on ITIL Version 2.0 (replaced in 2007 by Version 3) however, IMHO implementing Version 2.0 is a predecessor before attempting to implement a later version of ITIL. I've seen the process run like clockwork at a Fortune 500 organization and this book models the best support process I've seen in my 17-year IT career.

For a client, I chose Zendesk as the tool of choice because it was inexpensive and could meet most of the needs of the company. I've implemented multiple incident management and problem management processes and procedures with varying software solutions over the years and have seen both good results and good intentions gone wrong during that time.

There's never a solution that meets 100% of your needs, but this software met 95% of this company's major requirements, while solving many issues that an antiquated and expensive incident system was not solving.

This book will walk step-by-step in setting up each process, through a typical lifecycle of an incident.

Starting out, let's begin with definitions. Incident Management refers to the management of incidents and service requests. The goal of incident management is to resolve the incident as quickly as possible using any means necessary, including a workaround.

Incident: An unplanned interruption to an IT service or a reduction in the quality of an IT Service including failure of redundant services. The incident definition is also expanded to include Service Requests.

> Example: application error or infrastructure failure

Service Request: A request from a user for information, advice, standard change, or access to an IT Service.

> Example: 'How To' requests or requests for system administration changes

Problem Management refers to the management of problems and known errors.

The goal of problem management is to support incident management to resolve underlying cause of incidents, prevent incidents from recurring, identifying cause of past incidents, present proposals for improvement, and prevent recurrences by identifying infrastructure weaknesses.

Problem: An error in infrastructure which is the cause of one or more existing or potential incidents and root cause is unknown.

> Example: An out of memory exception on a server that causes failure of the software.

Known Error: a problem for which the root cause is known and for which a temporary workaround has been identified.

> Example: An application defect which has a workaround published which can be communicated to users.

Release Management refers to the goal of ensuring the successful rollout of a release including hardware and software.

Release Types:

Major: Significant rollout of new hardware/software and frequently eliminate known errors

Minor: Typically include a number of minor improvements and fixes to known errors

Emergency: Unplanned release to resolve a problem known error

Change Management refers to the approval and implementation of hardware and software changes. The goal of change management is to ensure that changes are implemented in a planned and authorized manner.

These processes integrate together to create a holistic software management and application management process.

The next page contains an overview of the process that will be created through this book.

ITIL Service Management

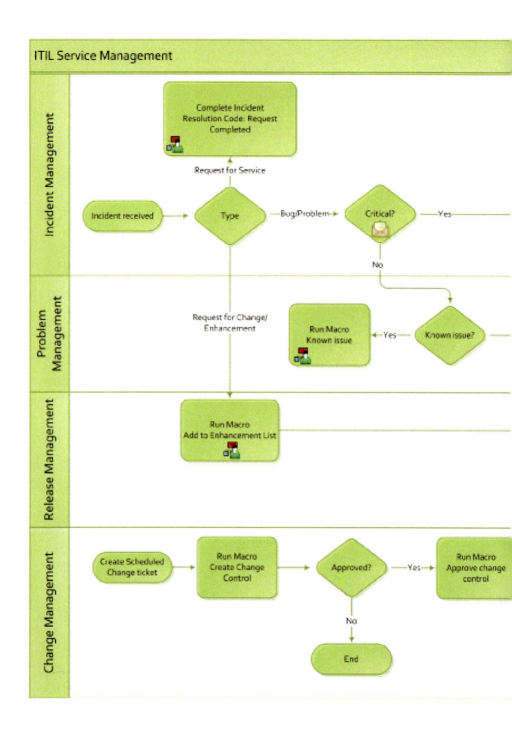

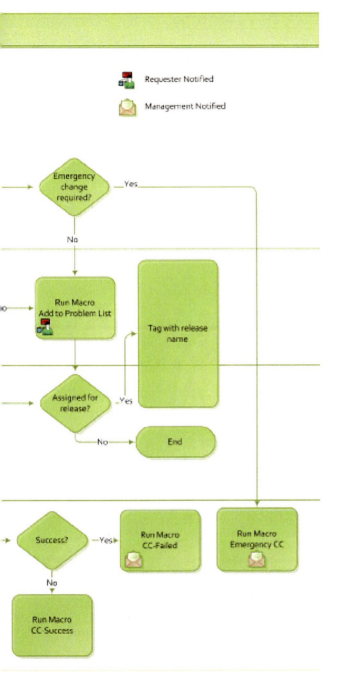

Requester Notified

Management Notified

Emergency change required?

Yes

No

Run Macro Add to Problem List

Tag with release name

Assigned for release?

Yes

No

End

Success?

Yes

Run Macro CC-Failed

Run Macro Emergency CC

No

Run Macro CC-Success

Zendesk out of the box does a pretty good job of performing incident management, but there are some configurations that need to be set up in order to fully support an end-to-end process, everything from priority notifications to tracking change controls and creating communications.

For the purposes of mapping Zendesk terminology to ITIL terminology, I've set up Zendesk with the following type of mapping:

Incident=Ticket

Request for Service=Task

Request for Information=Question

Request for Change (or Enhancement Request)=Task

Change Control=Task

Problem (or Defect)=Problem

The type and priority cannot be modified in Zendesk and the only modification in these fields is whether or not your organization supports 'On Hold' tickets. I recommend using this status for Problem Management and Request for Change type of items so the requester is aware of the status of their issue or request.

I'm using tasks instead of tickets for many of the categories since this allows me to create different SLAs for different types of ticket. A known issue or enhancement request in the system wouldn't have the same resolution time that a major outage would have, so by separating these into different the SLAs, this allows the organization to measure and meet expectations of the business.

Now that the ITIL foundation is established, let's begin.

Choosing the Edition

This book is created using the regular version of the software product but here are the primary differences between Regular and Enterprise:

1. The Enterprise version has a free "Light Agent" role that has the ability to view tickets, make private comments on the ticket, and view out of the box reports. Depending on your organization, you may want to choose the standard edition with more agents or the enterprise edition with many "Light Agent" roles.

2. Role support: The regular version supports three types of roles: User (free), Agent (at list price), and Administrator (at list price.) The enterprise version allows more support for different role types. For example, if you want certain groups to have access to certain macros, this is supported within the enterprise version.

3. Multi-brand support: If you want to create different portals and multiple branded sites through a central Zendesk setup, this is only supported through the enterprise version.

4. Business hours for SLA calculations is only supported through the enterprise version.

5. Multi-language support is only supported through enterprise or higher.

6. Ability to link tickets to known problems.

7. Advanced analytics (the out-of-the-box reporting only shows basic information about all tickets)

8. Custom themes for the Help Center

There are pros and cons to the cost vs. the benefits. In the company that I was consulting for, we opted for the regular version and it has worked to support their business needs at almost 20% of the cost of the enterprise license. The drawback to this is that any agent can assign tickets to any person listed as an agent (which in my case meant that I had one customer who started creating urgent tickets then assigning them directly to a developer to resolve and bypassed the process entirely.)

Setting Up Zendesk

Incident management is the beginning point and integration point into a number of other processes.

This process assumes that an item created in Zendesk has four different primary states: resolved (incidents and questions), defect (to be scheduled), enhancement (to be scheduled), or a change request (scheduled or emergency.)

Incident management is mostly set up in Zendesk, but there are some key items that I set up to take full advantage of the alerting, assignment, and macros that Zendesk provides.

Groups

In Zendesk, groups are used in place of queues that traditional incident management systems have. Groups are used to assign a ticket to a list of individuals, one of which takes the ticket and works to resolve it. Many IT organizations have an on-call rotation that monitors when tickets are assigned to the group, which makes it clear who is responsible for managing the ticket when it comes in.

Within Zendesk, there's a default support group that is created which is the default group that new requests are assigned to.

Groups are updated and maintained under the Admin->Manage->People menu. From there select add group to add new groups.

I created the following groups:

Support: This was created by default by Zendesk and is the first group that receives the request for triage. From there, it is either solved, or assigned to another group for review and resolution.

Change Management: This group is used to assign pending change requests for review and approval based on the Change Control Board (CCB) or sometimes called Change Advisory Board (CAB) schedule.

Infrastructure: Within the organization I am consulting for, this group is used to handle all infrastructure, hardware and desktop support requests. This type of group varies from organization to organization and may be multiple groups within an organization.

Problem Management: If an item is determined to be a defect in the system, this queue is used to group and bundle all open defects. If a duplicate is found, generally the duplicate is closed and the user is notified that the issue is a known issue. If it's a new issue, then sending to a Problem Management group allows you to review and prioritize all the open defects.

Once the ticket type is changed from incident to problem, then you have the ability to link the incidents to the problem ticket for tracking.

Product Management: If an item is determined to be an enhancement in the system, then this allows product teams to review the list of enhancement requests and determine when (or if) the request should be added to a product release cycle. Multiple groups may be required if multiple teams are responsible for this in your organization.

Support Escalation: This is a group that was created specifically for sending alerts when Urgent/High incidents are created.

Training: This is a group that was created specifically to handle 'question' tickets. Within the organization I am consulting for, they are responsible for customer and user training.

Even if you don't have these groups within your organization today, it's a good practice to tag and update the type to align with the type of request that was created.

By doing this, you can review the history of support over time to create analogous estimates of what might happen when rolling out a new software product or new enhancement release in your organization and prepare for changes.

Additionally, it's helpful to do this so you can manage to SLAs based on the type of ticket that are clearly defined with business stakeholders.

Adding Custom Fields

One of the powerful features of Zendesk is the ability to create custom fields.

The more fields you add, the more reporting you can do, but, the more difficult it is to fill out a ticket.

For simplicity's sake, I limited the custom ticket fields to add three new required fields.

1. **System:** This stores which application is having the issue. This contains the entire list of systems the team supports.

2. **Request Type:** This stored a request type to route the tickets automatically to different groups.

3. **Resolution Code:** this stores how the ticket was solved. I use this for reporting on the types of issues the team is getting. I use the following values:

   a. Change Control: The ticket required a system change to resolve.

   b. Config/Service Restart: The ticket required a configuration update or service restart to resolve.

   c. Data Update: The ticket required data to be updated to resolve.

   d. Defect: The ticket is a defect in the system.

   e. Enhancement Request: The ticket is an enhancement request in the system.

   f. No response: The ticket was closed due to a lack of response from the customer.

   g. Request Completed: The requested item in the ticket was provided.

   h. Training: The ticket is not an issue and more information was provided to the customer to resolve.

These resolution codes and groups are referenced in macros, triggers, and automations covered later in this guide so it's a good idea to set it up now.

You may want to add additional resolution codes but I'd argue for simplicity in this case. In every type of team, you get enough reporting and information from these resolution codes to determine how the bulk of your support is operating and where the team is investing their support time.

Setting Up SLAs

By default, all SLAs are disabled in Zendesk. The following are the SLAs that I configured that align to many ITIL implementations, however, these SLAs should be assessed based on the number of incidents and the capacity of the team to solve them to create realistic targets for resolution.

For each SLA, you can assign targets which are goals the team should be trying to achieve. 100% is unrealistic unless you have the team and processes in place to support 24x7 support. I'd recommend starting at 90% or 95% initially then creating team goals to increase this number over time.

I create SLAs for incidents only initially so that the team can get into the habit of what it means to have SLAs and to solve issues within a certain timeframe. People can 'game the system' by changing the type, however, that's easily corrected with the right reporting in place.

Here are the types of incidents and how they typically align to organizations:

Urgent: Urgent tickets are generally a 'System down' or global issue in which one or more mission-critical applications are down. These items generally must be assigned within 1 hour and solved within 4-8 hours, depending on the size of the organization and resources available.

High: High tickets are generally a system issue that affects an entire department or multiple users. These tickets also should have a short lifecycle with a resolution of less than 24 hours.

Normal: Normal tickets are routine tickets that should be assigned within 24 hours and resolved within 72 hours. In one implementation, we ended up implementing 5 days as the SLA for the regular license since business hours are not supported.

Low: Low tickets are also routine tickets that should be assigned within 24 hours and resolved within 5-10 business days, depending on your organization.

SLAs should have targets that are realistic for the team to accomplish.

Adding the On Hold Status

By default, On Hold is not set up within the Zendesk configuration. This is enabled by editing the Ticket Fields, select the Status field, and select the option to Add Status On Hold.

Drop-down field Status

Edit drop-down field

You are editing a **system ticket field**, so not all options on this page are editable.

For agents

Status

This is a system field, so you cannot edit the field title.

☐ **Required**

Field cannot be blank when an agent solves a ticket.

For end-users

☐ **Visible**

The field is visible to end-users on their ticket page.

Field options

☑ Add status On-hold

A ticket with status set to On-hold means that a response is needed from a third-party, not the requester or the assignee.
You can generate reports based on On-hold times. On-hold is included in the Requester Wait Time metrics, but not the Agent Wait Time metrics.
Enable this option to add On-hold as a ticket status.

Update field

Macros

Macros are used to standardize the process of categorizing data through tags and field updates.

By training agents to use Macros as their primary means of updating data in the system, you can automate a number of notifications and reporting within Zendesk.

Create new macros by navigating to Admin->Manage->Macros within Zendesk.

Most of the macros that come within Zendesk help the process of communication to agents and requesters in the system. I kept the default macros and added the following:

Assign to Training: This macro changes the type to question and assigned to the training group.

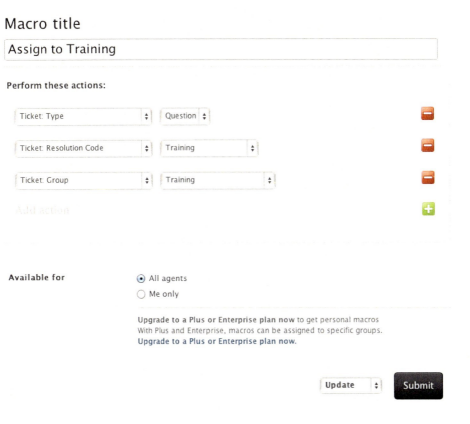

Macro title

Assign to Training

Perform these actions:

Ticket: Type ⬍	Question ⬍
Ticket: Resolution Code ⬍	Training ⬍
Ticket: Group ⬍	Training ⬍

Add action

Available for

⦿ All agents
◯ Me only

Upgrade to a Plus or Enterprise plan now to get personal macros
With Plus and Enterprise, macros can be assigned to specific groups.
Upgrade to a Plus or Enterprise plan now.

Update ⬍   Submit

Add to Enhancement List: This macro changes the ticket status to On Hold, changes the ticket type to task (which has different SLAs around it), assigns it to the Product Management group, then creates a standard email that communicates the enhancement process to the requester. You may want to automatically change the priority of the enhancement as a part of the process as well, depending on your organization.

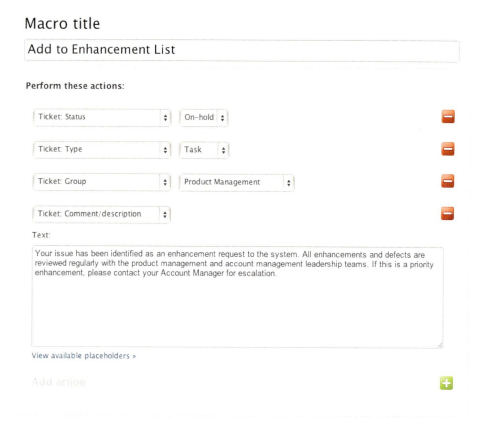

Macro title

Add to Enhancement List

Perform these actions:

Ticket: Status   On-hold

Ticket: Type   Task

Ticket: Group   Product Management

Ticket: Comment/description

Text:

Your issue has been identified as an enhancement request to the system. All enhancements and defects are reviewed regularly with the product management and account management leadership teams. If this is a priority enhancement, please contact your Account Manager for escalation.

View available placeholders »

Add action

Add to Problem List: This macro changes the status of the ticket to On Hold, changes the ticket type to problem, assigns it to the Problem Management group, then creates a standard email which communicates the defect process to the requester.

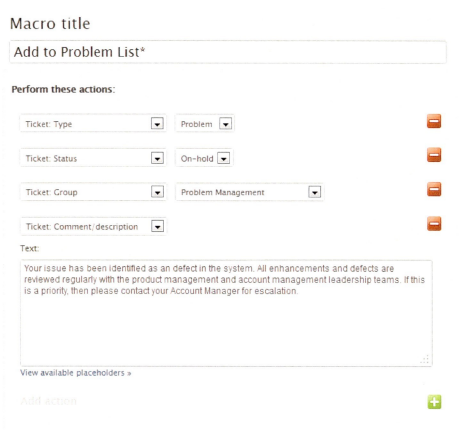

Macro title

Add to Problem List*

Perform these actions:

Ticket: Type	Problem
Ticket: Status	On-hold
Ticket: Group	Problem Management
Ticket: Comment/description	

Text:

Your issue has been identified as an defect in the system. All enhancements and defects are reviewed regularly with the product management and account management leadership teams. If this is a priority, then please contact your Account Manager for escalation.

View available placeholders »

Add action

Known Issue: This standard macro sends a standard message to an end user that this is a known issue in the system and to review the support documentation and sets it to resolved status. By default, it changes the ticket type to problem and the status to solved. I removed the process to change the ticket type to problem (which has different SLAs than incidents), and then updated the resolution code to defect. This allows me to track all support issues that are created for known issues in the system.

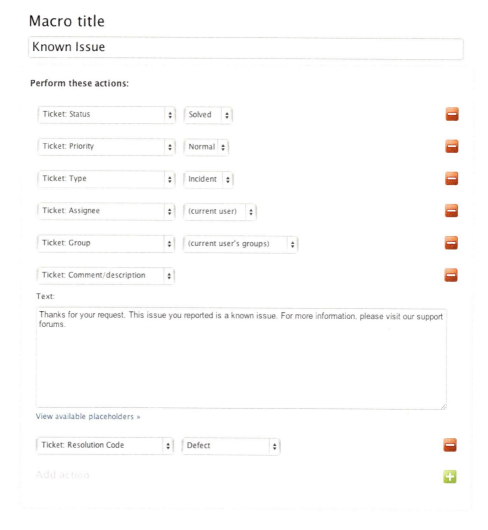

Create Change Control: This macro sets up the default description to be documented by the change owner and assigns the correct tags and groups to the task. It changes the type to task, resolution code to change control, the group to change management, sets a standard subject, and adds a tag for scheduled_cc.

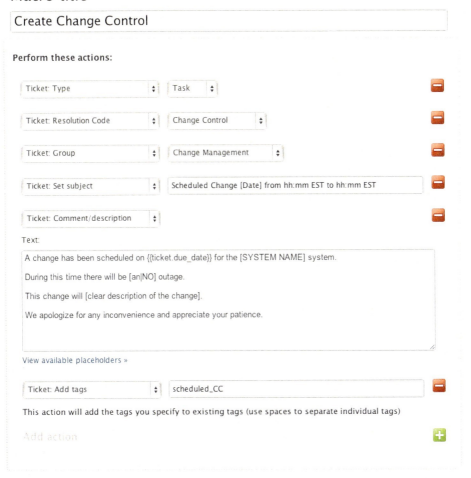

Macro title

Create Change Control

Perform these actions:

Ticket: Type | Task
Ticket: Resolution Code | Change Control
Ticket: Group | Change Management
Ticket: Set subject | Scheduled Change [Date] from hh:mm EST to hh:mm EST
Ticket: Comment/description

Text:

A change has been scheduled on {{ticket.due_date}} for the [SYSTEM NAME] system.

During this time there will be [an|NO] outage.

This change will [clear description of the change].

We apologize for any inconvenience and appreciate your patience.

View available placeholders »

Ticket: Add tags | scheduled_CC

This action will add the tags you specify to existing tags (use spaces to separate individual tags)

Add action

In our process, the change control steps are documented in an implementation plan that is attached to the change control and the description is very important in our process. We have an integration (covered in detail Advanced Integrations) that automatically creates a new priority article with the change control comments which appears on the customer support portal.

Submit for Change Control Approval: This macro assigns the ticket to the Change Management group and adds the tag scheduled_cc to the ticket.

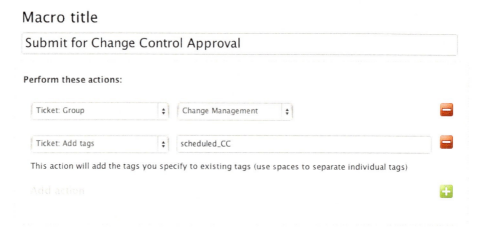

Macro title

Submit for Change Control Approval

Perform these actions:

| Ticket: Group | Change Management |
| Ticket: Add tags | scheduled_CC |

This action will add the tags you specify to existing tags (use spaces to separate individual tags)

Add action

Approve Change Control: This macro sets a tag called "approved" and creates an internal comment that the change control was approved.

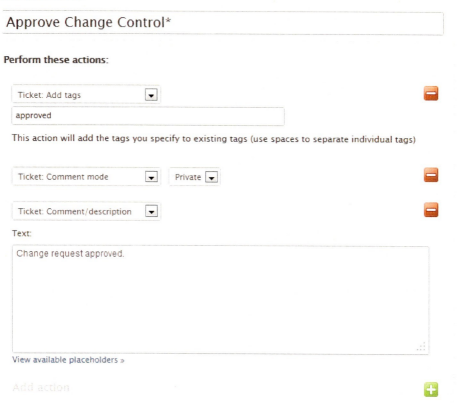

Macro title

Approve Change Control*

Perform these actions:

Ticket: Add tags

approved

This action will add the tags you specify to existing tags (use spaces to separate individual tags)

Ticket: Comment mode   Private

Ticket: Comment/description

Text:

Change request approved.

View available placeholders »

Add action

Emergency Change Control: This macro sets a tag called "emergency_cc", sets the resolution code to "Change Control", and creates a default internal comment with the description of the change.

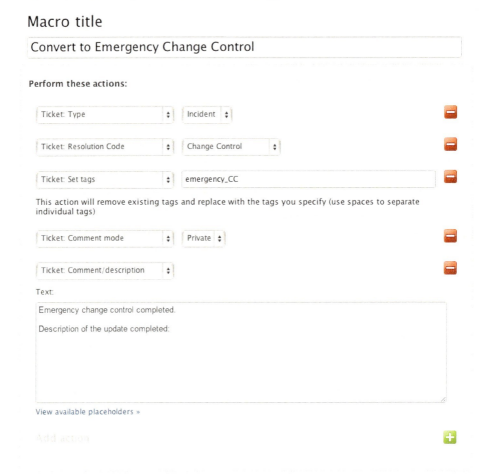

Macro title

Convert to Emergency Change Control

Perform these actions:

| Ticket: Type ⬍ | Incident ⬍ | ▬ |

| Ticket: Resolution Code ⬍ | Change Control ⬍ | ▬ |

| Ticket: Set tags ⬍ | emergency_CC | ▬ |

This action will remove existing tags and replace with the tags you specify (use spaces to separate individual tags)

| Ticket: Comment mode ⬍ | Private ⬍ | ▬ |

| Ticket: Comment/description ⬍ | | ▬ |

Text:

Emergency change control completed.

Description of the update completed:

View available placeholders »

Add action ➕

Triggers and Automations

A critical part of meeting SLAs rests on alerting. Setting up the right alerting allows management to get involved with the issue and manage it to completion.

There's nothing worse than the call from a senior executive asking 'Did you know that <insert mission critical system> is down?' and not being aware there was an issue.

Triggers and automations allow you to create key notifications for specific events that allow you to monitor and respond to a crisis.

The difference between triggers and automations are that triggers occur when someone saves an update to a ticket. Automations are time-based ticket updates or emails that occur after something has or has not happened within a specific time. We'll start with the triggers, then review setting up automations.

The out-of-the-box triggers send a number of email notifications to both the assignee and the requester. These triggers occur when the ticket is updated. These include notifications when the ticket is updated (both by the requester and the assignee), or when the ticket is reopened.

Triggers are maintained in the Admin->Business Rules section of Zendesk and allow you to modify ticket information or send emails when updates are made.

 kept all of the default triggers and added the following triggers:

New Ticket Defaults: This trigger automatically changes all new tickets to a Low Priority. In one organization I worked for, the default was 'Urgent' and as a result, almost 40% of their tickets were categorized as urgent. With hundreds of 'Urgent' requests, the team didn't know which items were actually urgent.

Additionally, enhancement requests, defects, support requests, and major projects were all tracked in the same system. Trying to get a priority on what to add to a release was a nightmare. Adding this rule became a critical way to help the team meet their SLAs.

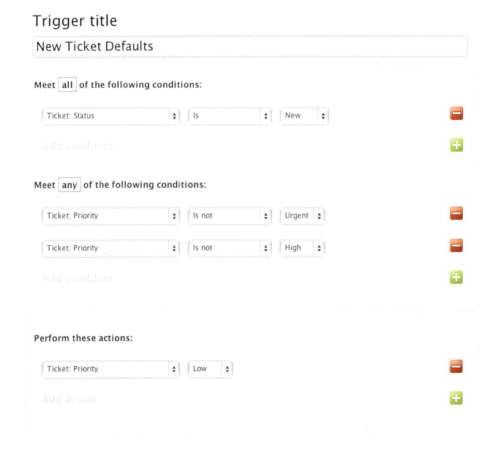

Notify Management of Priority Ticket: This allowed the management team to get an alert when a critical or high priority ticket was received so that the management team was aware and could manage the situation accordingly. This trigger sent an alert to the Support Escalation group whenever a new High Priority ticket was saved.

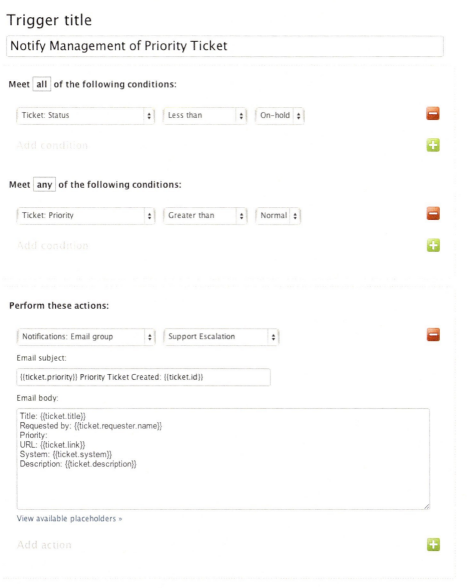

Trigger title

Notify Management of Priority Ticket

Meet all **of the following conditions:**

| Ticket: Status | Less than | On-hold |

Add condition

Meet any **of the following conditions:**

| Ticket: Priority | Greater than | Normal |

Add condition

Perform these actions:

| Notifications: Email group | Support Escalation |

Email subject:

{{ticket.priority}} Priority Ticket Created: {{ticket.id}}

Email body:

Title: {{ticket.title}}
Requested by: {{ticket.requester.name}}
Priority:
URL: {{ticket.link}}
System: {{ticket.system}}
Description: {{ticket.description}}

View available placeholders »

Add action

Notify Management of Emergency CC: By nature, with an emergency change control, the team fixes the issue, then fills out the change documentation later. This trigger (also using the same Support Escalation group) would email when a technician would set the Emergency CC values within the ticket (this was done through a macro.)

By creating this macro, this automates the notification so the management team was aware there was an issue and would enable the team to continue working the problem without taking the time to send out emails to IT management informing them of the issue.

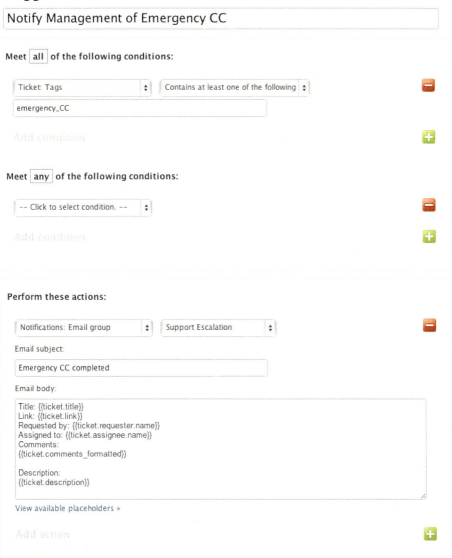

Trigger title

Notify Management of Emergency CC

Meet all **of the following conditions:**

| Ticket: Tags ⬍ | Contains at least one of the following ⬍ | ➖ |

emergency_CC

Add condition ➕

Meet any **of the following conditions:**

| -- Click to select condition. -- ⬍ | ➖ |

Add condition ➕

Perform these actions:

| Notifications: Email group ⬍ | Support Escalation ⬍ | ➖ |

Email subject:

Emergency CC completed

Email body:

Title: {{ticket.title}}
Link: {{ticket.link}}
Requested by: {{ticket.requester.name}}
Assigned to: {{ticket.assignee.name}}
Comments:
{{ticket.comments_formatted}}

Description:
{{ticket.description}}

View available placeholders »

Add action ➕

With the last two triggers created, I now have an automated notification system in place that emails in which key IT leaders when priority tickets are created or when emergency changes are completed.

Setting up Automations

Automations should be used for time-based updates and notifications. Note that you could create triggers and automations that create a loop of updates, so be careful not to add too many.

The following automations were created that assist with ticket maintenance and notifications:

Priority Ticket Alert – 1 Hour: This automation sends an email to the IT leadership group if a priority ticket is created and the status is not solved. (This automation can be repeated multiple times to alert management that the issue is not resolved.)

The priority ticket alert searches for all High or Urgent incident tickets (Greater than Normal) that are not solved and hours since created is 1. This sends an email to the leadership group that the issue is still open.

Automation title

Priority Ticket Alert – 1 Hour

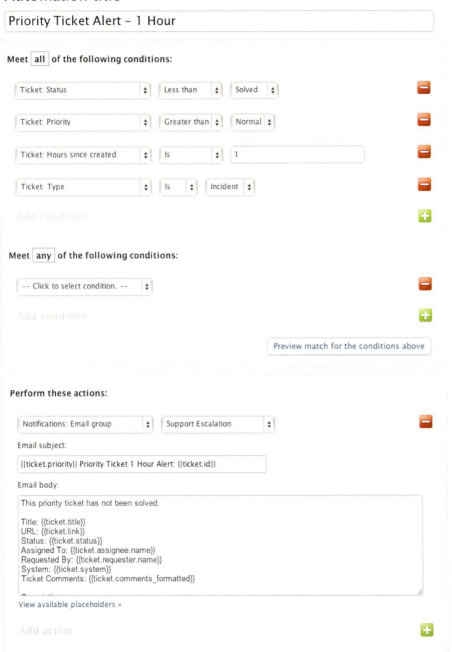

Meet `all` **of the following conditions:**

Ticket: Status	Less than	Solved
Ticket: Priority	Greater than	Normal
Ticket: Hours since created	Is	1
Ticket: Type	Is	Incident

Add condition

Meet `any` **of the following conditions:**

-- Click to select condition. --

Add condition

Preview match for the conditions above

Perform these actions:

Notifications: Email group   Support Escalation

Email subject:

{{ticket.priority}} Priority Ticket 1 Hour Alert: {{ticket.id}}

Email body:

This priority ticket has not been solved.

Title: {{ticket.title}}
URL: {{ticket.link}}
Status: {{ticket.status}}
Assigned To: {{ticket.assignee.name}}
Requested By: {{ticket.requester.name}}
System: {{ticket.system}}
Ticket Comments: {{ticket.comments_formatted}}

View available placeholders »

Add action

Pending Notification: This notification automatically sends an email to the requester if the status is changed to pending and the requester has not responded.

I have three different versions of the pending notification automation. One is the initial email after 3 days, the second is another reminder after 5 days that notifies the user that if they don't respond within 48 hours, then the ticket will be closed, the third sets the ticket status to solved, sets the resolution code to No Response, and sends an email that the ticket was closed due to lack of response.

Automation title

Pending notification 7 Days and Solve

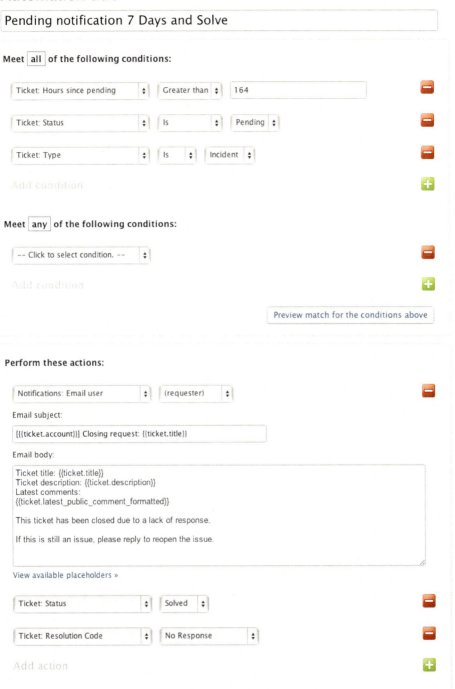

Meet all of the following conditions:

Ticket: Hours since pending	Greater than	164
Ticket: Status	Is	Pending
Ticket: Type	Is	Incident

Add condition

Meet any of the following conditions:

-- Click to select condition. --

Add condition

Preview match for the conditions above

Perform these actions:

Notifications: Email user | (requester)

Email subject:

[{{ticket.account}}] Closing request: {{ticket.title}}

Email body:

Ticket title: {{ticket.title}}
Ticket description: {{ticket.description}}
Latest comments:
{{ticket.latest_public_comment_formatted}}

This ticket has been closed due to a lack of response.

If this is still an issue, please reply to reopen the issue.

View available placeholders »

| Ticket: Status | Solved |
| Ticket: Resolution Code | No Response |

Add action

Setting Up the Help Center

The help center is a way that users can create support articles and a knowledge base that allow customers to search for solutions.

Once you enable the help center and select a theme, a number of default articles are created that have helpful information for setting up the portal.

There are two primary levels of information, public information and agent information.

Public information can be either open to the internet or, you can set up security so only users set up within Zendesk have access to the information. This will vary based on the type of support your company requires.

To effectively use the portal, you'll want to create a category first. Categories display on the home page of the portal which allow users to drill down to get more information.

To create a category, select Add Content from the Help Center editor and select Category.

generally create categories by application name or user role, depending on the types of users within the system.

Then create a section which is effectively a sub-category of information. I typically create three types of sections: Announcements, FAQ, Known issues, Training.

Announcements can be used for general announcements (priority issues, system outages, releases.)

FAQs can be used for the list of frequently asked questions on a site.

Known issues can be used to publish workarounds for known issues in the system.

Training can be used to publish training articles on the system.

From there, it's just a matter of adding an Article to a specific section and then populating content.

Reorder the sections by clicking Arrange Content and you are ready to go.

Advanced Integrations

Using Zapier to create Change Control notifications

Zapier is a third-party tool that can be used to integrate Zendesk with third party applications including CRM systems and email. At the time of this writing, pricing is $15/month and supports over 250 types of integrations.

Zapier can also be used to integrate Zendesk with itself.

In this case, I wanted to create a 'Zap' that if a Change Control was approved and had a notify tag in the ticket, then a new article would show up as a promoted article.

The first thing I did was created a view that contained the tickets that would meet the criteria for notifications. (Status is Open, Type was Task, Tags: cc_scheduled, approved, notify).

Adding the notify tag helps to verify that the item should be published as an article.

View title

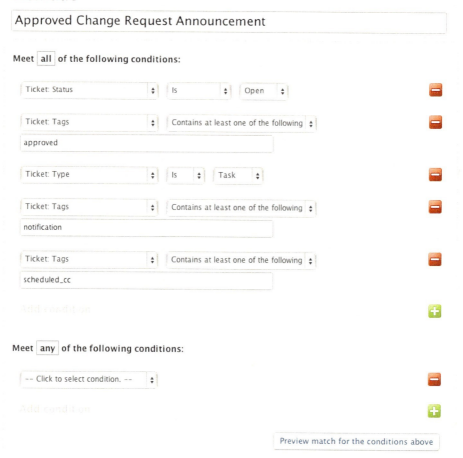

Then I created a zap that pulled the tickets in the view, then created a new article within Zendesk with the information from the ticket. When a new ticket is created, then create a topic.

Then select the filter that was created in Zendesk.

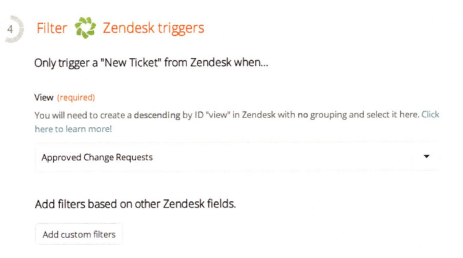

And then select the information that needs to be created in the topic.

5 Match up  Zendesk Ticket to Zendesk Topic

Forum ID (required)

Forum that the topic is associated to

Announcements ▼

URL (optional)

The API url of this topic

Insert ⚙ fields

Title (required)

The title of the topic

System Change Scheduled

Insert ⚙ fields

Body (required)

The unescaped body of the topic

A system change has been scheduled. Description

Insert ⚙ fields

Topic Type (optional)

The type of topic. Either "articles", "ideas" or "questions"

articles

Insert ⚙ fields

Submitter ID (optional)

The id of the user who submitted the topic

Insert ⚙ fields

Updater ID (optional)

The id of the person to last update the topic

Insert ⚙ fields

Locked (optional)

Mark "true" or "false" to determine if comments are allowed

false	Insert ⚙ fields

Pinned (optional)

Mark as "true" or "false" to determine if the topic is marked as pinned and hence eligible to show up on the front page

true	Insert ⚙ fields

Highlighted (optional)

Set to "true" to highlight a topic within its forum

true	Insert ⚙ fields

This created an article automatically with the information in the ticket!

FAQs

So now that you've implemented Zendesk, here's some FAQs when just starting out using Zendesk.

How do I Export Tickets to Excel?

Open a View with the tickets that require export, click the down arrow next to the view name, and select Export as CSV.

What's the easiest way to add new users?

1. You can upload a list of users into Zendesk.

2. If you have 'Anyone can submit tickets' enabled in the Settings->Customers section, then users are automatically added when they send an email to your support email account (this automatically creates a new end user account in Zendesk.)

3. If you have the previous setting in step 2 enabled and the 'Enable email forwarding' set in the Settings->Agent section, you can forward an email to your Zendesk support email account and the user account will be created.

Note that organizations aren't automatically created, but, if the email domain from an existing organization matches the new user's email domain, they will be automatically added to that organization.

How do I print a ticket?

Open the ticket, at the bottom of the page is Ticket Options. Select Print Ticket from there.

How do I merge two tickets?

Open the ticket options and select merge into another

icket.

How do I create confidential tickets?

This isn't really supported in Zendesk at the time of this writing. Forums tell you to add a confidential checkbox, then remove them from views, however, these tickets are still visible through searches and if users have access to all tickets in their organization, they can view tickets there. You may want to set up another Zendesk instance and link the two accounts for these types of issues.

How do I assign assets to users?

Customize the user fields to add asset information.

How do I allow users to see tickets created by other people in their organization without giving them an agent account?

User accounts have two types of permissions when editing the user, to view their own tickets (default) or to view all tickets in their organization.

Conclusion

Zendesk is a powerful tool with some great options. Between using Zapier to integrate and the native functionality, it becomes easy to integrate and update information throughout a ticket lifecycle.

44490654R00029

Made in the USA
Middletown, DE
08 June 2017